SHELLEY FAYE LAZAR'S
ORIENTAL COLLECTION

SHELLEY FAYE LAZAR'S
ORIENTAL COLLECTION

20 ORIGINAL NEEDLEPOINT DESIGNS

PHOTOGRAPHY BY GUS FILGATE

Charles E. Tuttle Company, Inc.
Boston · Rutland, Vermont · Tokyo

First published in the United States in 1993 by
Charles E. Tuttle Company, Inc. of Rutland, Vermont & Tokyo,
Japan, with editorial offices at 77 Central Street, Boston,
Massachusetts 02109.

Library of Congress Catalog Card Number 92–63363

ISBN 0–8048–1849–5

Designed by Janet James
Technical Editor Judith Casey
Stitch diagrams by Kate Simunek
Assistant needleworkers Mrs. Chris Kerby and Mrs. Edna Cousins
Typset by Florencetype Limited
PRINTED IN SPAIN

Please note that all materials specified in this book should be available
from good craft shops and yarn stores.

CONTENTS

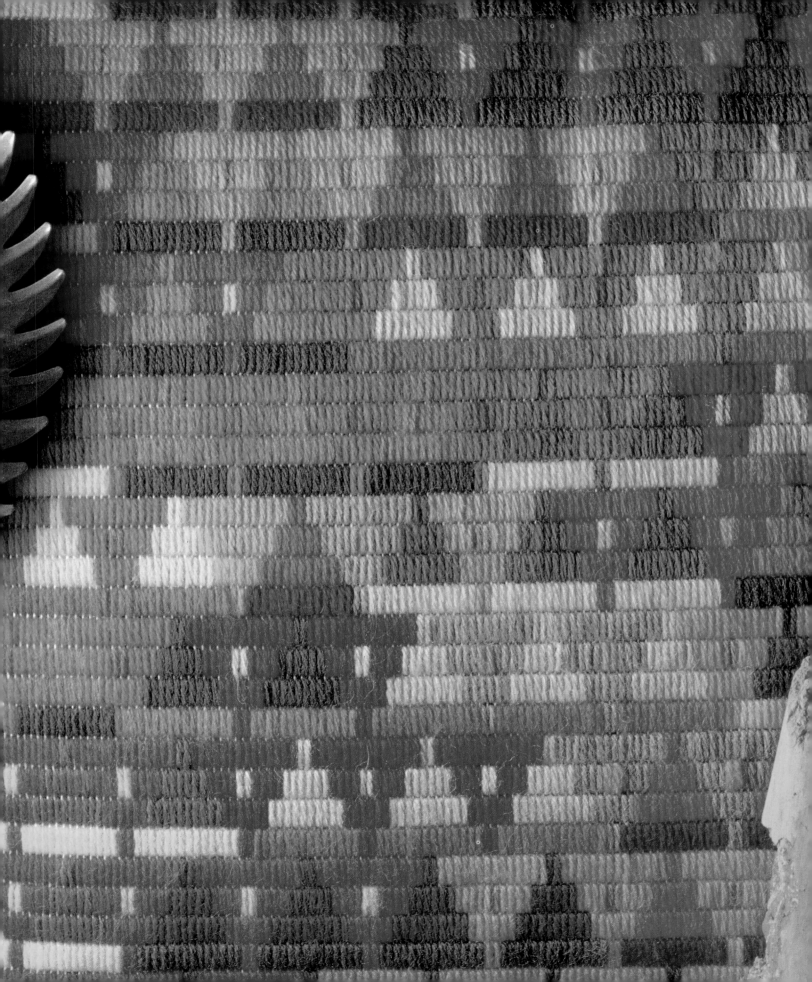

FOREWORD

Travelling through India and Asia, I could not help but absorb the vibrant and exciting stimuli. Colours, shapes and designs became new and alive under the brilliant canopy of constant blue skies. Throughout my journey, colour seemed to fuel my search for more and more inspiration. Sometimes a simple motif on a textile could set me off developing a design in needle and thread. At other times, visual elements simply

offered themselves to be translated directly and immediately onto canvas. I also found that where textiles, embroidery and design had social significance, as well as decorative use, they offered further creative interest. ❧ Some designs I could visualize instantly on canvas, in a particular thread and stitch. Other designs seemed to evolve from a variety of elements absorbed unconsciously, slowly filtering out to produce some surprising and enjoyable results. ❧ I hope these twenty designs will be an interesting pictorial guide to the places I visited and that you will be able to share in the excitement I felt, by sewing the designs yourself. I hope it will also inspire you to consider your experiences as a source for your own needlework designs.

INTRODUCTION

CANVAS

All the designs in this book use interlock canvas of 10, 12 or 14 threads to 1in (2.5cm), with the exception of the Chinese Chequers rug design which uses an interlock canvas of 7 threads to 1in (2.5cm). Each design gives the amount of canvas including a margin of about 2–3in (5–8cm) around the design to be stitched. This allows for mounting the completed tapestry or making it into a cushion, and also stretching and handling whilst sewing.

THREAD

A range of threads has been used in these designs, taking into consideration the most suitable yarn for the design, canvas and stitch. Experimentation is the key and I hope, by making your own adaptations, you will produce interesting variations.

Persian 3-stranded yarn

The Persian stranded yarn I have used comes in 170yd (155m) long, 4oz hanks. Hanks are useful when you need a large quantity of one colour for one area. Also available for smaller areas are 8yd (7.3m) skeins. The number of strands you use can be altered to suit the design, stitch and canvas.

Tapestry yarn

The tapestry yarn I have used is a 4-ply twisted yarn available in 9yd (8.2m) skeins or in some colours as 42.7yd (39m) hanks. It is a useful yarn for both tent stitch and straight stitch on 10- and 12-mesh canvas; thick enough to cover the canvas thread completely but not so thick as to make stitching difficult.

Soft embroidery cotton (retours)

This is a fairly thick soft thread with a matt finish available in 10yd (9m) skeins.

Coton perlé (pearl cotton)

This is available in skeins of various thicknesses. Coton perlé 3, which I have used in the Tropical Fish and Bagh Chal designs, comes in skeins of $27^3/_8$yd (25m). Coton perlé 5, used in the Nepalese Fire Dragon and the Aboriginal Tales designs, is available in $52^1/_2$yd (48m) balls or $27^3/_8$yd (25m) skeins. It is a twisted cotton with a lustrous finish which gives a contrast to yarn or soft cotton.

Gold thread

Metallic yarns, sometimes called goldfingering, may be more readily found in your supplier's knitting section. The thicker yarn comes in large balls, while the thinner yarn is available in spools. If only the thin variety is available, simply use the thread doubled.

NEEDLES

For needlepoint, use a needle which has a rounded point. They are available in a range of sizes and throughout I have specified the most suitable size. The selection is governed by the mesh of the canvas – the needle should pass through the hole easily without distortion – and, at the same time, by the thickness of the thread – it should go through the eye of the needle and should not fray during stitching.

STRETCHER FRAMES

Ideally you should mount your canvas on a frame so that the canvas is evenly stretched and remains so while working the design. Artist's canvas stretcher frames are available in pairs to any length and therefore can be made up to any square or rectangular shape. Staple, pin or tack the canvas centrally to the frame. Other frames that can be used are:

Needlepoint floor frame. Available in various widths, this frame is useful because it stands by itself and can be positioned at various heights and angles.

Needlepoint threaded side hand frame. This has adjustable wooden sides and is available in various widths. As with the artist's canvas stretcher frame, it requires some support so as to free both hands for stitching.

Needlepoint rotating frame. Available in various widths, this has a depth of 12in (30cm) so that only one area of a design can be worked at any one time. The advantage of this type of frame is that it is more portable.

USING THE CHARTS AND DIAGRAMS

The designs in this book are either charted on graphs or given in line drawings with guidance for colour selection. A caption beside each chart indicates the stitch required and the number of threads over which it is sewn. When working from a complex graph, you may find it easier to follow if you first enlarge it on a photocopier.

Where the design is given as a line drawing, divide the drawing into a grid with sections using vertical, horizontal and diagonal lines. Scale up the design to full size onto another sheet of paper before transferring the design to the canvas. Alternatively, you could enlarge the design on a photocopier until you reach the correct size. To transfer the design to the canvas, lay it over the design and trace the outlines using a pale felt-tip pen or soft pencil.

STITCHING

For the stitch instructions, please refer to the illustrated stitch section at the back of the book. Never use too long a length of thread otherwise it will twist and wear thin before it is finished. Experience teaches you the most suitable length to use.

At the start of stitching, push the needle and thread through the canvas on the front (right) side, a little distance from the area you are about to work. When your stitches cover the thread, trim off the loose end. To fasten off a length of thread, darn it through previously-made stitches on the reverse (wrong) side of your work. Avoid using knots to secure the

INTRODUCTION

thread because they can cause bumps in the finished article.

It is not advisable to make a needlepoint stitch in just one movement, especially if the canvas is stretched on a frame. (For the purposes of illustration only, diagrams show a stitch being made all in one movement.) To make the stitches correctly, use the 'two hand' method. Insert the needle down through the canvas with the hand on top of the frame, and pull the needle through with the hand below the frame. Push the needle back up with the hand below the frame and pull through with the hand on top. With practice and speed, you can achieve a regular stitch. Keep the tension even by not pulling the thread too tightly.

BLOCKING

If you have worked your tapestry on a frame, your canvas should still be square. However, you may find there is some distortion which needs to be straightened out before you can frame your work or make it into a cushion.

To block your work you will need a thick piece of board. Draw an accurate grid on one side. Varnish the board to avoid the wood staining the canvas when dampened. Lightly spray the back of the canvas with water – a plant spray is ideal. Then, starting at two opposite sides, secure the canvas to the board, with the right side down, using a staple gun or nails. The grid allows you to align the canvas squarely. Secure at ½in (1cm) intervals until the two sides are in place. Secure the other two sides in the same way. Leave the canvas to dry away from sunlight for about three days.

COMPLETION OF FINISHED ARTICLE

The completed needlepoint can be sewn into a cushion or mounted on board as a wall hanging.

To make a cushion

Cut a piece of backing fabric to the same size as the canvas, including the margin. With right sides together, stitch fabric and canvas around the edges, close to the tapestry and leaving a large enough gap for turning through and inserting a cushion pad. Clip the corners and turn the cover to the right side. Insert the pad and slipstitch the gap neatly to close it.

To mount the needlepoint

If you plan to frame your tapestry after it is mounted you need to choose the frame first. Measure the part of the frame moulding that will overlap the edge of the tapestry. This is known as the rebate. Then cut a piece of hardboard to the size of the tapestry plus the width of the rebate all round. Place the tapestry, right side up, centrally on top of the hardboard. Turn under one edge of the canvas and pin it to the hardboard using panel pins inserted into the thickness of the board. Pin the opposite edge in the same way. Then, using strong thread, lace the two edges together working stitches diagonally. Fasten securely, remove panel pins and pull the lacing taut. Secure the other two sides of the canvas in the same way.

Important note

Measurements are given throughout in both inches and centimetres. Please note that the first measurement given is always the height and the second measurement is the width.

THE DESIGNS

◆

O N E

SCALES OF THE DRAGON

Thailand is a country of many colours and contrasts. The mysterious temples, called 'wats', have entrances guarded by growling dragons with fierce teeth, whose bodies snake up the stairways. At each wat the dragons are different, giving a foretaste of the riches to be found within. The simple yet beautiful pattern created by the dragons' scales provided me with the initial inspiration for this design. To avoid the monotony of making a whole cushion cover in just two or three colours, I decided to weave in some additional interest. ✿ Bangkok is a lively and varied city, and there is much more beyond the Royal Palace and the temples. One day, I also went to see a floating market, where a variety of local produce is sold upon the maze of waterways. There I was offered (for a price) some locally-made, painted bamboo hats, and I couldn't resist the colourful patterns they created, piled up in the boat. ✿ In this design I combined the colours of the hats with the shapes of the dragon scales.

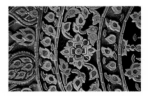

The brilliant details found within the Royal Palace and in the guardian dragons challenged me to design with an equally exotic variety of colour.

SCALES OF THE DRAGON

FINISHED SIZE

16in (41cm) square

MATERIALS

20in (50cm) square of 10-mesh canvas
Size 20 needle

Tapestry yarn: two hanks each in ecru and white; three skeins each in cerise, pink, bright red, brick red, ochre, yellow, bright green, forest green, turquoise, blue, mauve and purple (or a combination of your own choice).

STITCHING

The design is worked in straight stitch of varying lengths. Find the approximate centre of the canvas and work the first scallop following the chart for the length of each stitch. Each square on the chart represents one horizontal canvas thread. When the first scallop is complete, work outwards from the centre, one scallop at a time. To give an even tension over the whole canvas, sew one row at a time, alternately at the top and the bottom. Insert the needle into the canvas where a stitch has already been made, so that the needle does not come up against a stitch and pull the thread.

It is not necessary to follow my colour scheme or distribution of colour but, if you are using your own colours, be sure that they make a well-balanced composition.

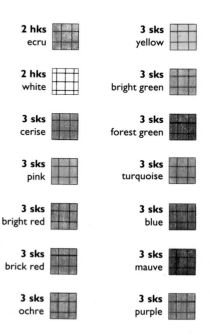

2 hks ecru	**3 sks** yellow
2 hks white	**3 sks** bright green
3 sks cerise	**3 sks** forest green
3 sks pink	**3 sks** turquoise
3 sks bright red	**3 sks** blue
3 sks brick red	**3 sks** mauve
3 sks ochre	**3 sks** purple

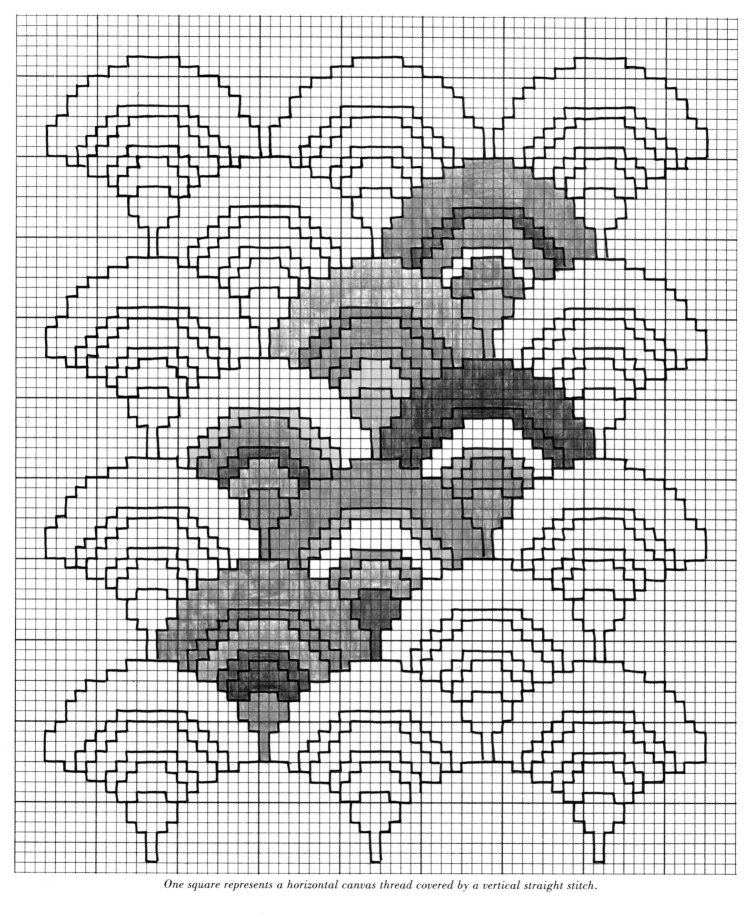

One square represents a horizontal canvas thread covered by a vertical straight stitch.

TWO

TROPICAL FISH

Sit on the beach in Lovina in Bali and the locals will swarm around you like bees at a honey-pot. Little children try to sell you pineapples, ladies offer massages and colourful batik sarongs, and young boys want to practise their English. One offer which I succumbed to was a boat trip to a small coral reef for some snorkelling. The black sand of Lovina beach made the crystal-clear sea appear unusually dark and threatening, but under the sea a completely new world opened up. So many wonderful fish in unimaginable colours appeared, as if straight out of a child's colouring book. These creatures, which belong more in the realm of fantasy than reality, were the inspiration for this design. It would be impossible to capture all their marvellous colours, so I just had fun with the sizes and shapes of the fish I recalled. The simplicity of the design sets off the brilliant blues of the sea and the sky.

Bali has idyllic scenery and a wonderful atmosphere.
Fish-headed boats ward off evil sea spirits and lead to
underwater mysteries and inspiration.

TROPICAL FISH

FINISHED SIZE

16in (41cm) square

MATERIALS

20in (50cm) square of 14-mesh canvas
Size 22 needle

Soft cotton (retours): twenty-four skeins of pale aquamarine and two skeins of dark aquamarine (for the sea); eight skeins of bright blue (for the sky); one skein each of pale yellow, three shades of green (for the land and trees), and brown.

Coton perlé 3 (pearl cotton) (for the fish): one 27³⁄₈yd (25m) skein each of bright red, purple, pale aquamarine, grass green, violet, blue, bright pink, purple-pink, orange, yellow, lemon, turquoise, black, and ecru.

STITCHING

The sea and the sky are worked in tent stitch, using the basketweave method. This method can be very useful when working large areas of one colour as slight variations in the dye-lots create a subtly shaded effect. It also causes less distortion to the canvas. Each square on the chart represents one stitch, which is a tent stitch, or half cross stitch, worked over two intersecting canvas threads.

Begin by working the sun, sky and island using soft cotton (retours) in yellow, bright turquoise, shades of green, and brown. Centre the island in the top quarter of the overall design. Work about ¹⁄₂in (1cm) of dark aquamarine for the sea immediately around the island.

Now stitch the fish using coton perlé (pearl cotton) which gives an extra sheen. Follow the charts, using any combination of colours and fish. When there are enough fish to make a pleasing composition, fill in the remaining area of sea using the pale aquamarine soft cotton (retours).

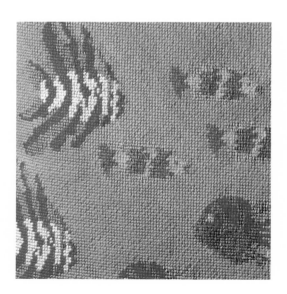

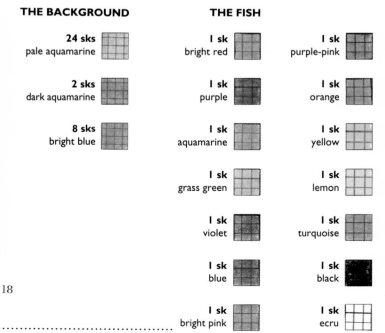

THE BACKGROUND

24 sks pale aquamarine	
2 sks dark aquamarine	
8 sks bright blue	

THE FISH

I sk bright red		**I sk** purple-pink	
I sk purple		**I sk** orange	
I sk aquamarine		**I sk** yellow	
I sk grass green		**I sk** lemon	
I sk violet		**I sk** turquoise	
I sk blue		**I sk** black	
I sk bright pink		**I sk** ecru	

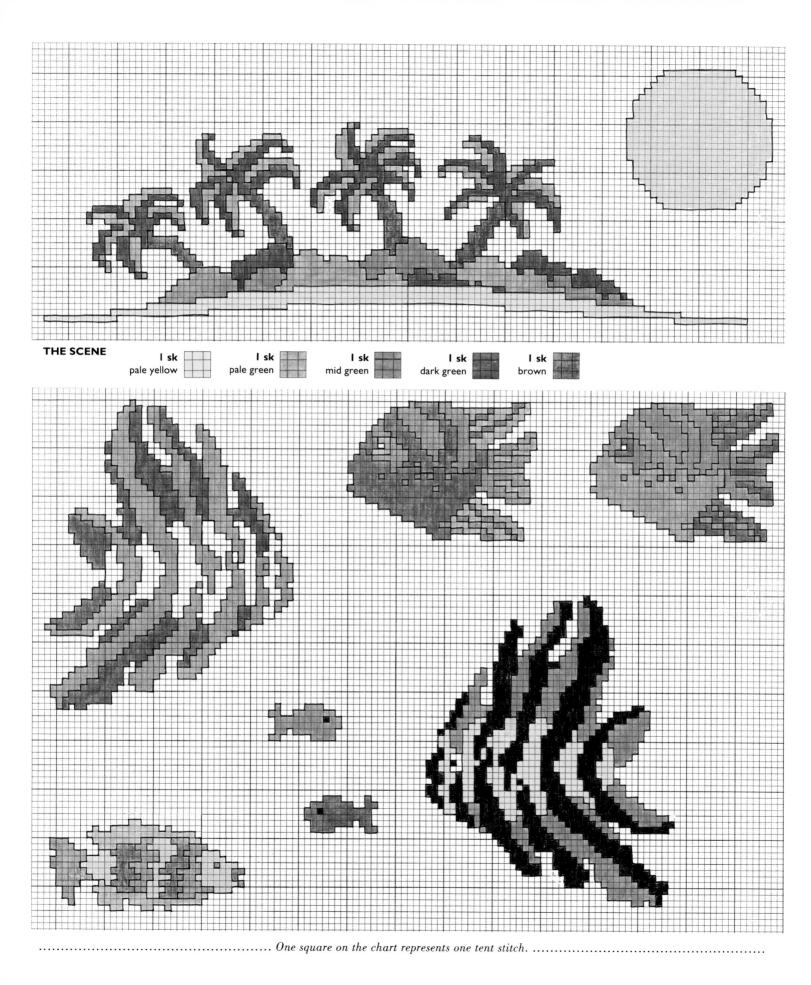

THE SCENE

I sk pale yellow	**I sk** pale green	**I sk** mid green	**I sk** dark green	**I sk** brown	

One square on the chart represents one tent stitch.

◆

MYSTICAL MASK

Bali is a very mystical island with many symbolic customs. Although I seldom understood their significance, I could enjoy the spectacle, such as the stone thrones adorned with black-and-white chequered cloth, flowers and fruits. ⚜ Masks play a very important part in Balinese culture, both in religious activities and in dances. Carved out of local wood, masks represent gods or demons. Some look very human and others are gruesome monsters, with undertones of strength and foreboding. One mask in particular was very simple and graphic and I knew it would translate well into needlepoint. To balance the primary colours of the mask and to add weight to the design, I used the black-and-white chequered pattern that I had seen on the cloths to make a strong border.

The masks and symbolic offerings evade interpretation
by casual onlookers like me but, nonetheless, entertain,
delight and inspire.

MYSTICAL MASK

FINISHED SIZE

16in (41cm) square

MATERIALS

20in (50cm) square of 10-mesh canvas
Size 20 needle

Tapestry yarn: two hanks in each of black and white; skeins in the following amounts and colours: seven dark green; four yellow; three pink; two each of dark blue, bright red, purple, grass green, orange; one skein of blue-grey.

STITCHING

This design uses tent stitch for the mask and diagonal stitch for the chequered border. Measure out the area of the finished design from the centre of the canvas. Count twenty threads in from the edge of the design to allow for the black-and-white border.

Transfer the mask image onto the canvas by dividing the canvas into sixteen squares and scaling up the chart onto the canvas. Draw in the black outlines of the design. (The lines are not strictly symmetrical, to give a softer effect.)

Stitch the mask outlines in black yarn, then simply fill in the coloured areas. Use the basketweave method of tent stitch as the areas of colour are quite large. Once completed, stitch the chequer border using black and white thread alternately. Each black or white square on the border covers five vertical and five horizontal threads and should be worked in diagonal stitch.

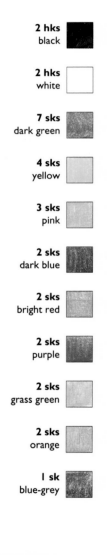

2 hks black	
2 hks white	
7 sks dark green	
4 sks yellow	
3 sks pink	
2 sks dark blue	
2 sks bright red	
2 sks purple	
2 sks grass green	
2 sks orange	
1 sk blue-grey	

The mask area is sewn in tent stitch using the basketweave method. Each black or white square on the border is stitched in diagonal stitch over an area of five horizontal and five vertical threads.

FOUR

NEON LIGHTS

In Hong Kong the most modern Western technology meets the most ancient customs of the East. This tapestry does not attach itself to any specific sight in Hong Kong, but to the memory and overall impression that remains with me: Hong Kong Island; the business area; neon lights reflected in the water at night; the feeling that business was going on twenty-four hours a day. ❧ The design is shown here in two colourways. The original remains closest to my memory of a pitch-black sky with bright, primary coloured neon lights and brilliant gold stars.

Inspiration can come from surprising sources – here it was the spectacle of modern architecture and vivid colours mirrored and distorted on the water.

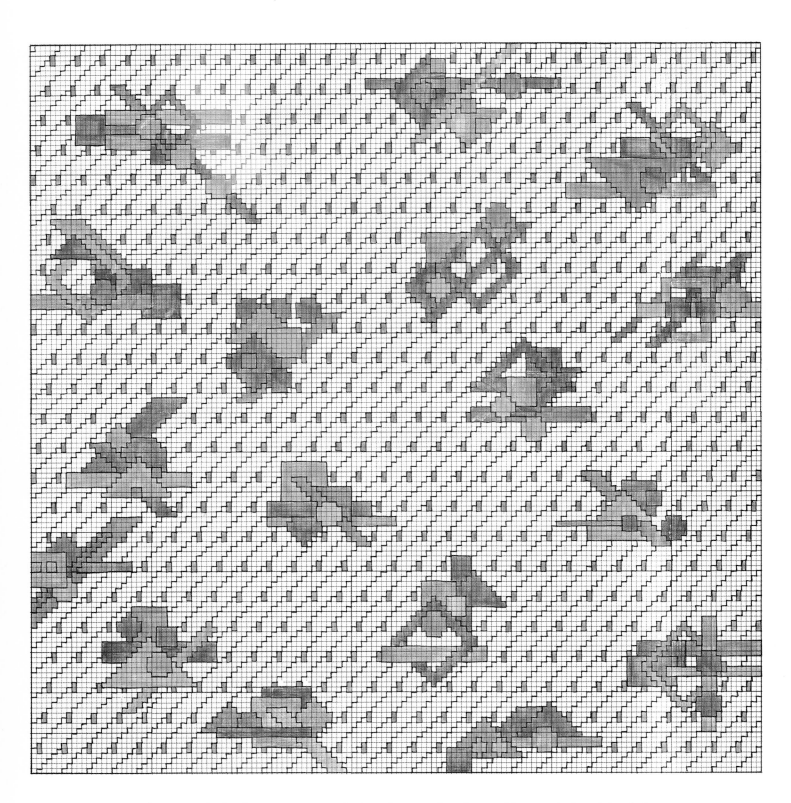

One square in the chart represents one horizontal canvas thread covered by a vertical straight stitch.

NEON LIGHTS

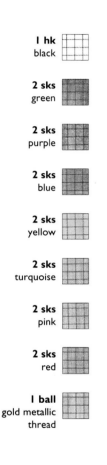

I hk
black

2 sks
green

2 sks
purple

2 sks
blue

2 sks
yellow

2 sks
turquoise

2 sks
pink

2 sks
red

I ball
gold metallic
thread

FINISHED SIZE

14in (36cm) square

MATERIALS

16in (41cm) square 10-mesh canvas
Size 18 needle
Tapestry yarn: one hank in black; two skeins each of green, purple, blue, yellow, turquoise, pink, and red; one ball of gold metallic thread.

STITCHING

The chart shows the arrangement of the coloured neon motifs set against the black background, but their position is not crucial. You can play around with the arrangements and colours as desired.

Each square on the chart represents one horizontal canvas thread. Start by sewing the background colour in diagonal bands over five horizontal canvas threads, noting that every sixth stitch is worked over only three canvas threads to allow for a gold stitch worked over two canvas threads. When you reach a coloured motif, break the diagonal lines and complete the motif from the chart before continuing the background.

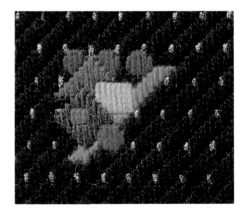

BHUTANI JIGSAW

Kathmandu is a city of contrasts, with modern goods such as videos and pizzas on sale just around the corner from narrow streets of three- and four-storey houses that haven't changed in centuries. These dark, mysterious streets hold the enchantment of Kathmandu. The combination of Indians, Tibetans, Chinese and Nepalese provides a wealth of riches and colour, reflected in the wide variety of textiles and paintings. My attention was taken by an Indian trader who specialized in textiles from Bhutan. (Bhutan borders Nepal, sandwiched between Bangladesh and China, and is very difficult for the ordinary traveller to visit.) The 'Bhutanis' he sold were large cloths, wonderfully embroidered, and they provided me with the inspiration for this design. I studied their patterns and found that the designs locked together like a jigsaw in panels. So, likewise, the same patterns begin and end this design and in between there are blocks fitted together and repeated, but using different colours.

The textile shop attracted me like an Aladdin's cave. The exciting designs and colours echoed my desire to use vivid wools.

BHUTANI JIGSAW

FINISHED SIZE

17in (43cm) square

MATERIALS

20in (50cm) square of 10-mesh canvas
Size 20 needle
Tapestry yarn: five skeins each of orange and bright red; four skeins each of magenta-pink and turquoise; two skeins each of lemon, dark green, bright green, blue-green, burgundy, gold, lime-green, bright blue, pink, salmon, purple, emerald, mauve, and yellow.

STITCHING

The design is worked using straight stitch throughout over two horizontal threads. Refer to the key (below left) to see where each block is placed. Starting at the base of the design, follow the charts to sew one block at a time, noting the changes of colour as you go.

It is important to follow the charts closely in order to reproduce this design, but it is not necessary to keep to my colour combinations. Your choice of colour will make the design unique to you!

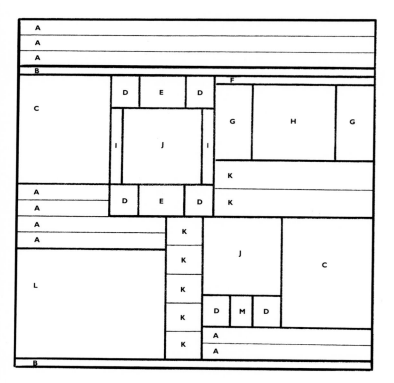

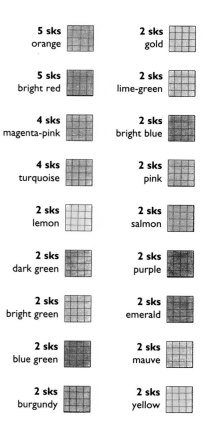

5 sks orange

2 sks gold

5 sks bright red

2 sks lime-green

4 sks magenta-pink

2 sks bright blue

4 sks turquoise

2 sks pink

2 sks lemon

2 sks salmon

2 sks dark green

2 sks purple

2 sks bright green

2 sks emerald

2 sks blue green

2 sks mauve

2 sks burgundy

2 sks yellow

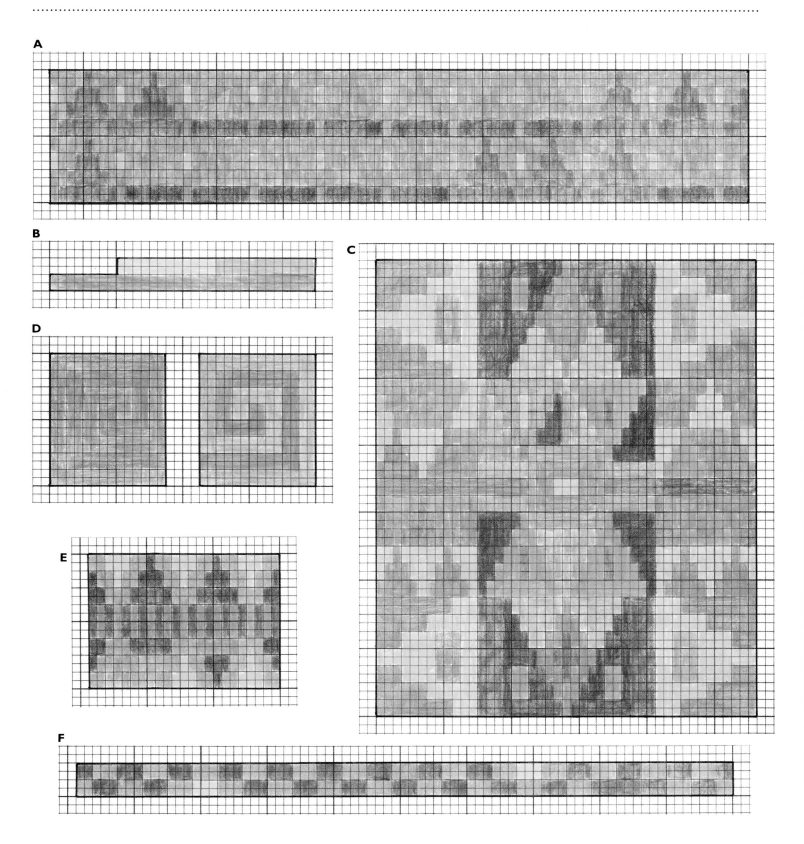

*In the charts, each square represents one horizontal
canvas thread covered by a vertical straight stitch.*

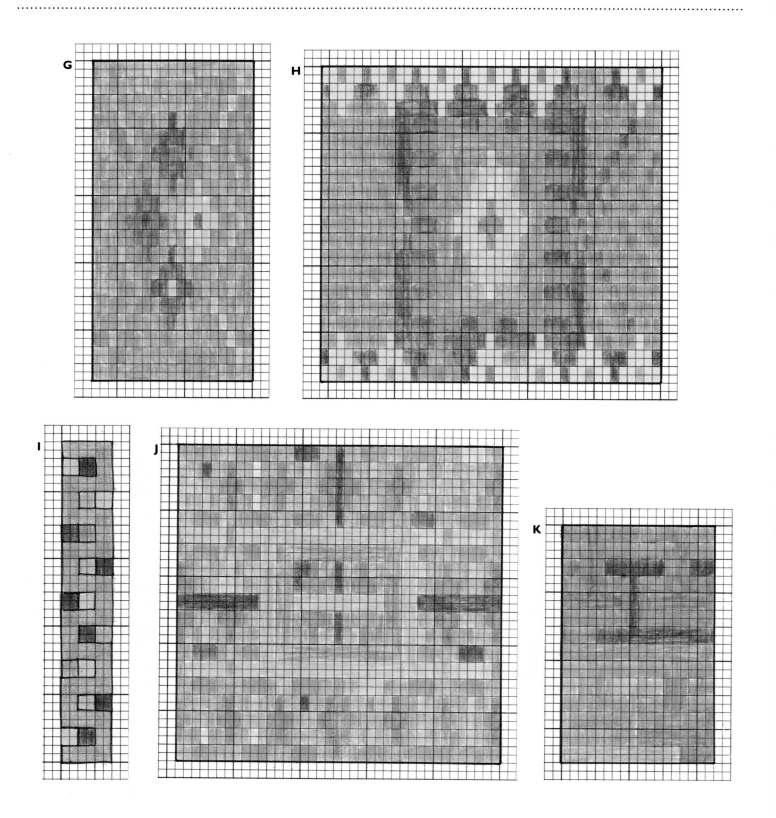

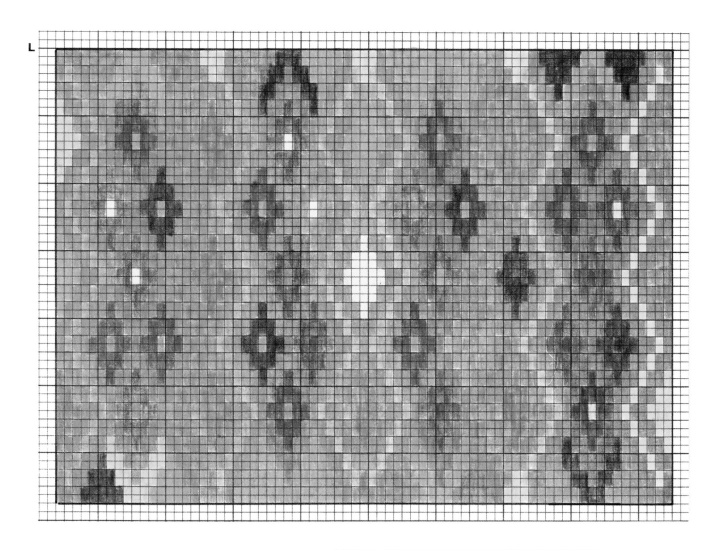

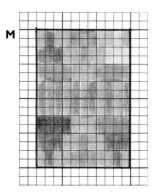

MYSORE RAINBOW

In the Indian city of Mysore the air is filled with a strong scent which emanates from the sandalwood carvings and incense. Mysore's main attraction for me is its colourful night market. It's like stepping into a child's kaleidoscope – even the display of plastic buckets shouts colour at you. There are stalls selling vivid powder dyes, each cone-shaped display of colour more shocking than the last. The stall-holders' wonderful arrangements of colours and shapes were the inspiration for this design. The same colours and cone-shaped motifs are featured in the Nepalese Bhutani cushion so that the two complement each other.

I travelled to Mysore specially to see the market, to absorb and be ignited by the brilliant display of colour in every direction.

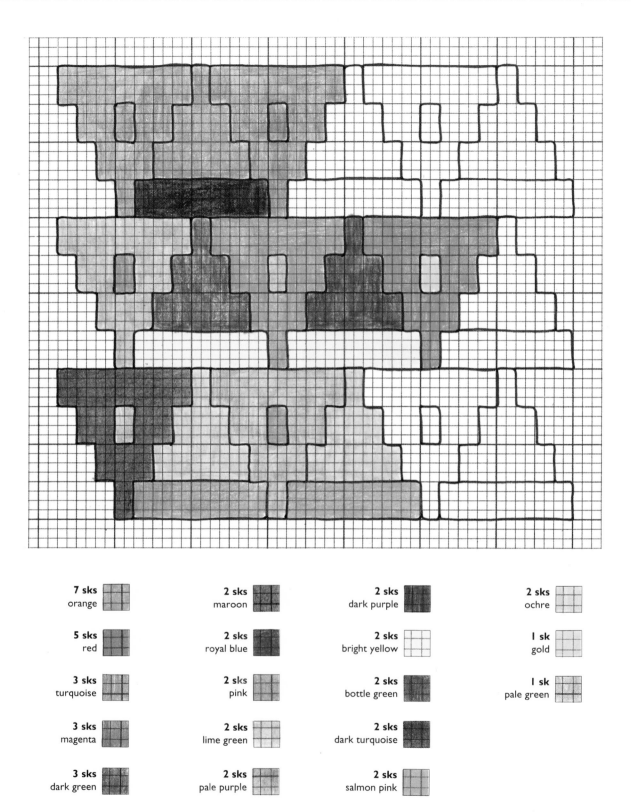

7 sks orange	**2 sks** maroon	**2 sks** dark purple	**2 sks** ochre
5 sks red	**2 sks** royal blue	**2 sks** bright yellow	**1 sk** gold
3 sks turquoise	**2 sks** pink	**2 sks** bottle green	**1 sk** pale green
3 sks magenta	**2 sks** lime green	**2 sks** dark turquoise	
3 sks dark green	**2 sks** pale purple	**2 sks** salmon pink	

In the chart, each square represents one horizontal canvas thread covered by a vertical straight stitch.

MYSORE RAINBOW

FINISHED SIZE

17½in (44.5cm) square

MATERIALS

22in (56cm) square of 10-mesh canvas
Size 20 needle
Tapestry yarn in the following amounts and colours: seven skeins of orange; five skeins of red; three each of orange, turquoise, magenta, dark green; two each of maroon, royal blue, pink, lime green, pale purple, dark purple, bright yellow, bottle green, dark turquoise, salmon pink, ochre; one each of gold and pale green.

STITCHING

This design is very straightforward, using straight stitch over four canvas threads throughout. The chart shows a section of the pattern and the construction of the 'cones'; each square on the chart represents one horizontal canvas thread. Begin at the centre of the canvas and work outwards, stitching rows alternately at the top and the bottom to keep an even tension. Wherever possible, work into a hole where a stitch has already been made, so that the needle does not come up and pull a thread.

You can either follow my colour arrangement or make up your own, but try to plan the distribution of colour evenly throughout to give a balanced composition.

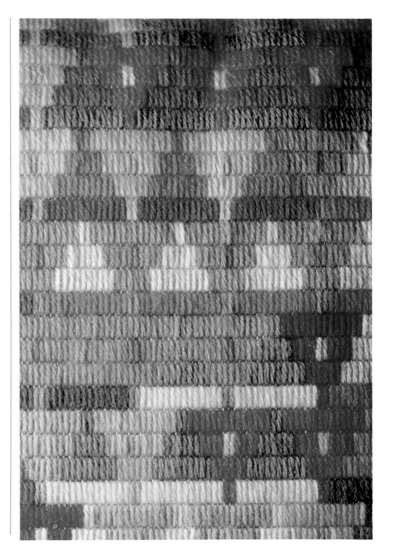

FLORAL BATIK

Indonesia is the home of the batik printing process. In simple terms, batik involves making a wax impression on fabric which is then dyed. The waxed areas of the fabric do not take the dye and the design is thereby revealed. There are many different regional designs and colours, which also have social significance. ❧ I went round several 'batik factories' and watched with fascination as the material evolved through the various dyeing and printing processes to produce the finished article. The copper stamps that transfer the wax pattern onto the fabric are works of art in themselves. I took several impressions of the stamps and based my design on one of them. I selected colours which I felt were typical of the finished batiks – bright and cheerful combinations against a dark background.

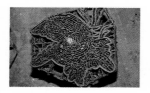

The copper batik stamps are used to create intricate patterns that are repeated over and over again on lengths of cotton.

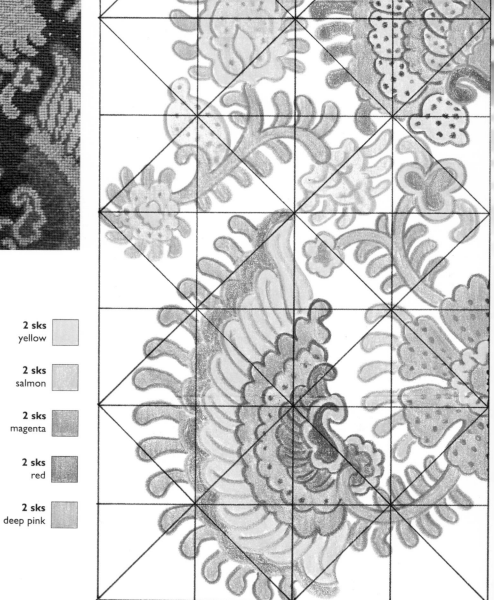

I hk
dark blue

2 sks
pale green

2 sks
bright green

2 sks
forest green

2 sks
turquoise

2 sks
bright purple

2 sks
purple

2 sks
yellow

2 sks
salmon

2 sks
magenta

2 sks
red

2 sks
deep pink

The design is worked in tent stitch.

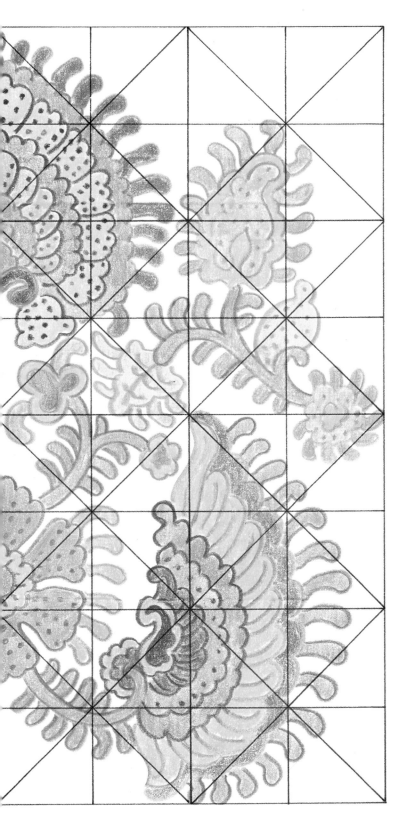

FLORAL BATIK

FINISHED SIZE

15in (38cm) square

MATERIALS

19in (48.5cm) square of 14-mesh canvas
Size 22 needle
Persian 3-stranded yarn: one hank of dark blue; two skeins each of pale green, bright green, forest green, turquoise, bright purple, purple, white, yellow, salmon, magenta, red and deep pink; gold thread.

STITCHING

Divide the canvas in half and draw the design onto one half following the line drawing. Transfer the design section by section for optimum accuracy.

Starting at the centre, stitch the outline of the shapes you have marked. Use two strands of yarn throughout and work in tent stitch. Stitch the corresponding other half of the design at the same time to ensure that it stays completely symmetrical.

When the main design is complete, work the gold stitches at regular intervals (every five threads) across the background and then fill in the remaining areas with dark blue using the basketweave method of tent stitch.

EIGHT

TIGER, TIGER

Woven tiger rugs originate from Tibet and are extremely rare. They were used for travel and as seating rugs, although their deeper significance remains shrouded in mystery. As the rugs emerge from the hidden world of Tibet, the various designs are a source of great enjoyment. I was introduced to the tiger design when I went to a Tibetan camp in Nepal, where rugs are made for export and for the tourist industry, and I saw a modern tiger rug amongst the geometric and floral designs. ❧ As well as trekking in the Himalayas, I was privileged to visit the National Reserve Park of Chitwain. At 5am each morning, I sat on the back of an elephant for a dawn jungle trek. On one of these excursions we found a tiger's nest with two newly born tiger cubs and on another I saw two fully grown tigers. Using the Tibetan rugs as inspiration, I decided to celebrate my good fortune in seeing these relatively rare creatures with a needlepoint design.

TIGER, TIGER

FINISHED SIZE

33 × 19in (84 × 48.5cm)

MATERIALS

35 × 21in (89 × 53.5cm) 12-mesh canvas
Size 20 needle

Tapestry yarn: four hanks of ecru; two hanks each of pale green, ochre and black; nine skeins of dark orange; four skeins of orange; two skeins of pale yellow; one skein each of pink, red, pale blue, stone, white, emerald, beige, dark red, blue and green.

STITCHING

Transfer the line drawing to the canvas with a soft pencil or pale felt-tip pen. The entire design is in straight stitch of varying lengths over horizontal canvas threads, following the lines of the drawing. Begin by stitching the black details of the tiger. Then fill in the canvas with dark orange, orange and ochre. Then work the tail, paw and face details in the remaining colours. Avoid making very long stitches by dividing the length into two shorter stitches.

The background is a lattice effect created by interwoven diagonal bands of straight stitch.

One square on the chart represents one horizontal canvas thread. The diamonds created are filled in with a subtle, pale green yarn.

The 'fringe' at the top and bottom of the design, called 'rainbow pattern' by the Tibetans, reflects their love of colour and also has symbolic meaning. The blocks of colours cover ten horizontal canvas threads in a series of five vertical stitches.

As with most of the designs in this book, the tiger can be made as a small picture or as a luxurious, large rug by using a different-sized canvas mesh and the appropriate thickness of thread, and stitch.

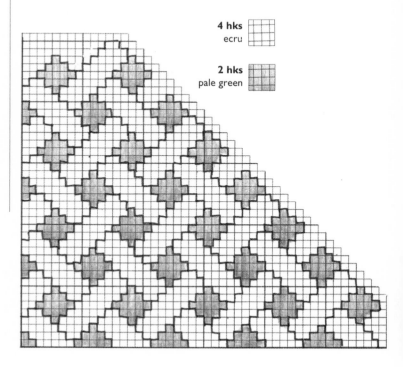

4 hks ecru

2 hks pale green

The entire design is sewn in vertical straight stitch of varying lengths. The chart above shows the background design, where each square represents one horizontal canvas thread covered by the straight stitch.

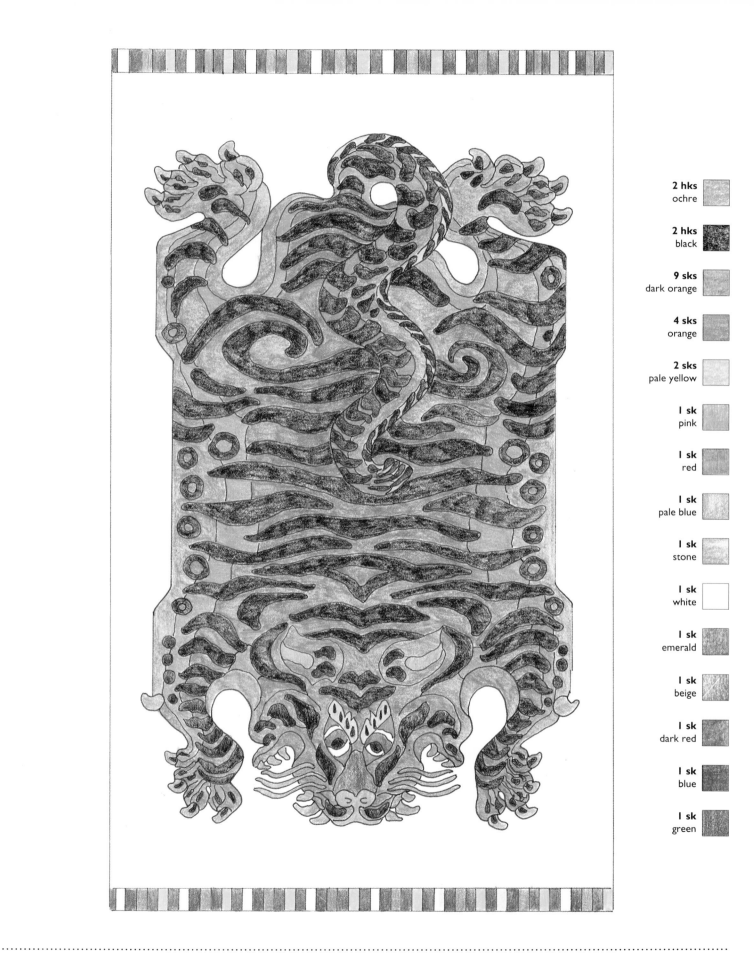

2 hks
ochre

2 hks
black

9 sks
dark orange

4 sks
orange

2 sks
pale yellow

1 sk
pink

1 sk
red

1 sk
pale blue

1 sk
stone

1 sk
white

1 sk
emerald

1 sk
beige

1 sk
dark red

1 sk
blue

1 sk
green

TEMPLE PAINTINGS

I returned to the Madurai temples, after an all too brief first visit, to study the wonderful wall paintings of the Shree Meensakshi Temple which dominates the skyline of Madurai. The temple even has its own bazaar, making a walled city within a city. The multicoloured images in this place alone could be the inspiration for a wide range of designs. ❧ I was drawn to the circular paintings on the ceilings of the labyrinthine corridors, finding that their geometric designs made a change from the usual visual representations of gods and animals. I selected just one of them and simplified it, while retaining the essence of its design. Although the colours would originally have been much brighter, I decided to use muted primary colours to reflect the paintings in their present state. I was particularly interested in the use of shadow in the Indian paintings, which I included in my design to give a three-dimensional effect.

It was easy to become lost in the corridors of the temple by studying the geometric designs painted on the ceilings and walls.

TEMPLE PAINTINGS

FINISHED SIZE

13in (33cm) diameter circle, or finished square

MATERIALS

16in (41cm) square of 12-mesh canvas
Size 20 needle
Persian 3-stranded yarn: one hank bright blue; two skeins each of white, pale blue, pale blue shadow, yellow, yellow shadow, bright green, red, dark red shadow, bottle green, grey, dark brown, tan.

STITCHING

The design is worked in tent stitch throughout using two strands only of the Persian yarn. The circle is divided into four symmetrical quarters, except for the central flower motif as shown in the chart. Stitch the central motif first and then work outwards, completing each segment of the design before starting the next to ensure accuracy. Work the background in tent stitch using the basketweave method.

If you prefer the finished design to be a circle, omit the background, reducing the quantity of bright blue yarn to two skeins.

I hk bright blue	
2 sks white	
2 sks pale blue	
2 sks pale blue shadow	
2 sks yellow	
2 sks yellow shadow	
2 sks bright green	
2 sks red	
2 sks dark red shadow	
2 sks bottle green	
2 sks grey	
2 sks dark brown	
2 sks tan	

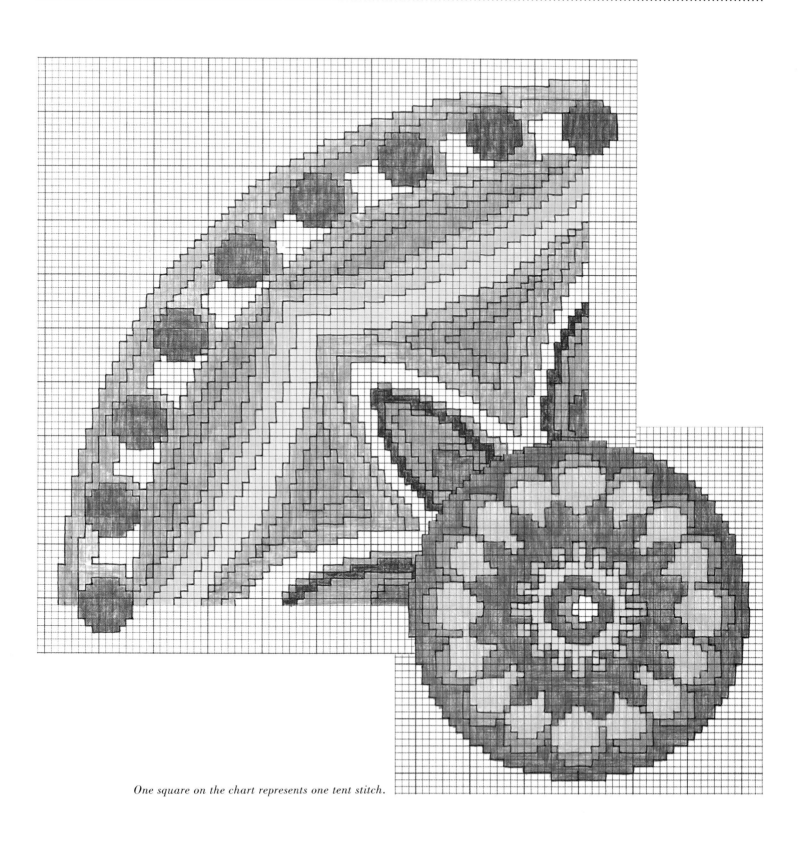

One square on the chart represents one tent stitch.

TEN

PIPLI UMBRELLAS

Pipli is a small community in the Orissa region of north-east India. I reached the village by a curious combination of transport, but it was worth it just to see the spectacle of a road lined with shops selling wall hangings and temple umbrellas in unbelievably bright colours. Pipli is renowned for its appliqué work, produced by the menfolk and passed on from generation to generation. It is in fact quite crude, but the effect is very striking and leaves an everlasting impression. I created this design using various elements from the villagers' appliqué work, extending the range of shades to make it even more colourful.

A combination of elementary shapes and vivid primary colours make these umbrellas a wonderful, instructive example of how simple designs can be stunning.

Pipli Umbrellas

FINISHED SIZE

14½in (37cm) diameter circle, or finished square

MATERIALS

17in (43cm) square of 10-mesh canvas
Size 18 or 20 needle

Persian 3-stranded yarn: one hank of white; five skeins each of green and red; three skeins of orange; two skeins each of blue, turquoise, pink, lemon and purple; one skein of brown. (You will only need five skeins of white for the circular version.)

STITCHING

Using tent stitch throughout, follow the design from the chart and work from the centre outwards, completing each ring of the design before starting the next. Each square on the chart represents one tent stitch on the canvas.

The finished design can be circular or filled out to make a square. Work the background in tent stitch using the basketweave method.

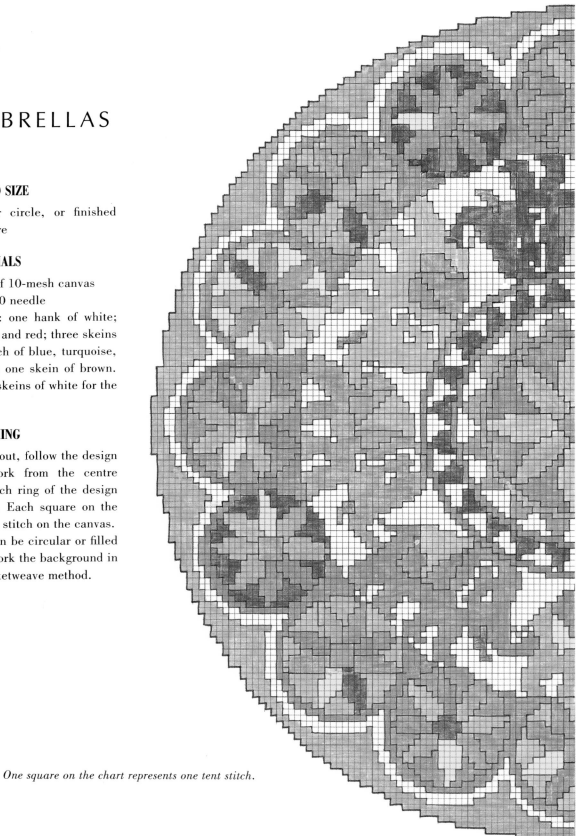

One square on the chart represents one tent stitch.

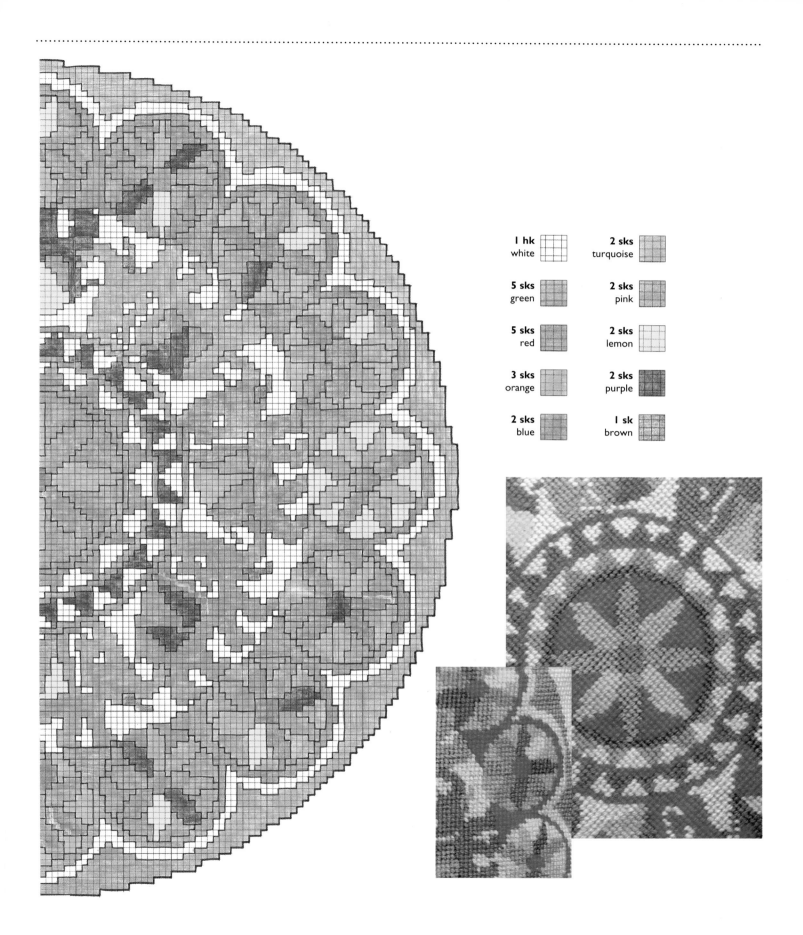

1 hk
white

5 sks
green

5 sks
red

3 sks
orange

2 sks
blue

2 sks
turquoise

2 sks
pink

2 sks
lemon

2 sks
purple

1 sk
brown

◆

ELEVEN

EYES OF THE STUPA

'Stupas' are Nepalese Buddhist temples, built on hilltops, where religious icons and prayer wheels and prayer flags can be seen. At these high points are bronze towers, painted with pairs of imposing, watchful, all-seeing eyes. These eyes are a very strong feature of life in Kathmandu and, embroidered on jeans and T-shirts, almost become the city's logo. ☘ For my design I concentrated on the eyes, but I wanted also to keep an impression of their setting. The red, green, blue and yellow diamonds represent the fluttering prayer flags. (When the flags are blown by the wind, the prayers printed on them are surrendered to the elements and borne up to the gods.) The four coloured bands above the eyes add to the visual interest. The ochre bands suggest the bronze towers and the blue bands remind me of the brilliant April skies of Kathmandu.

The stupas, built up from basic shapes and colours, emphasize the power and depth of the eyes painted on the towers.

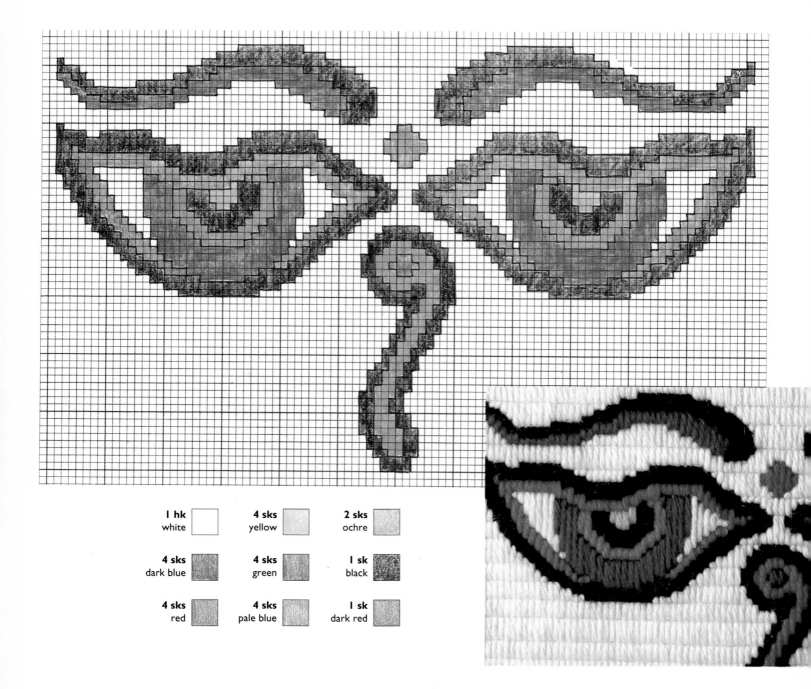

1 hk white		**4 sks** yellow		**2 sks** ochre	
4 sks dark blue		**4 sks** green		**1 sk** black	
4 sks red		**4 sks** pale blue		**1 sk** dark red	

EYES OF THE STUPA

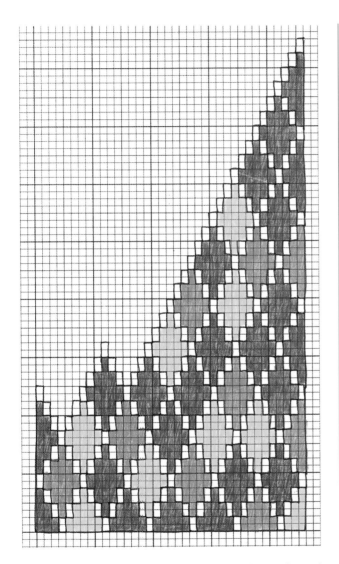

In these charts for the eyes and side panels, each square represents one horizontal canvas thread covered by the vertical straight stitch.

FINISHED SIZE

14 × 15in (36 × 38cm)

MATERIALS

18 × 19in (46 × 48cm) of 12-mesh canvas
Size 20 needle
Tapestry yarn: one hank of white; four skeins each of dark blue, red, yellow, green, pale blue; two of ochre; one skein each of black and dark red.

STITCHING

This design is extremely simple, sewn in straight stitch over horizontal canvas threads. Each square on the charts represents one horizontal canvas thread. Mark a 2in (5cm) border around the edge of the canvas. Begin by sewing the dark red dot between the eyes, placing it in the centre of the canvas, 9in (23cm) up from the lower border. Following the chart, complete the eyes and nose.

Next, work the horizontal bands of white, ochre and light blue below the eyes. The length of the stitch varies from row to row, adding visual interest and tonal effects. The four bands of red, blue, green and yellow above the eyes are all the same depth – worked over five canvas threads.

Sew the side borders, working the lattice of white straight stitches first, according to the chart, where each stitch is worked over two horizontal canvas threads. Then fill in the diamonds, distributing the colours randomly. The diamonds are worked in straight stitch over two/six/twelve/six/two canvas threads.

BAGH CHAL

This is a game that obsesses Nepalese people of all ages. They can be seen playing it absolutely anywhere, using almost anything as a board and pieces. 'Bagh Chal' means 'move the tigers'. The central motif and borders reflect traditional designs found in Tibetan and Nepalese rugs. ⚑ The needlepoint makes a good table decoration or, of course, you can simply use it to play 'Bagh Chal'.

HOW TO PLAY 'BAGH CHAL'

The board consists of a network of lines with twenty-five intersecting points. One player has four tigers and the other has twenty goats. The players take it in turns to place the four tigers (which are always placed in the four corners at the beginning of the game) and four of the goats on the board. The goat player then continues to place the goats on the board in an attempt to block in the tigers, while the other player moves a tiger one space at a time and can 'eat' the goats by jumping over them one by one. When all the goats are on the board they can then be moved one space at a time. The game is won when the tiger has eaten five goats, or when the goat player encircles the tigers to prevent them from moving.

BAGH CHAL

FINISHED SIZE

11in (28cm) square

MATERIALS

15in (38cm) square of 12-mesh canvas
Size 20 needle
Soft cotton (retours): four skeins each of orange, turquoise and white; two of red; one of green.
Coton perlé 3 (pearl cotton): four 27⅜yd (25m) skeins of white
70 gold beads; invisible thread; fine needle

STITCHING

The design is worked throughout in cross stitch and each stitch, represented by one square on the chart, is worked over two horizontal and two vertical canvas threads. Make sure that the top diagonal stitch always lies in the same direction.

Starting at the centre of the canvas, work outwards in all directions, leaving the white areas till last. The white areas inside the 'board' design are worked in coton perlé (pearl cotton), the rest of the design is in soft cotton (retours).

When the cross stitching is complete, sew the gold beads to every third stitch on the yellow border, as shown. To use the design as a table mat or games board, simply mount the tapestry over hardboard.

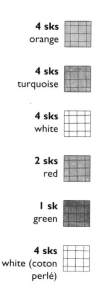

4 sks	orange
4 sks	turquoise
4 sks	white
2 sks	red
1 sk	green
4 sks	white (coton perlé)

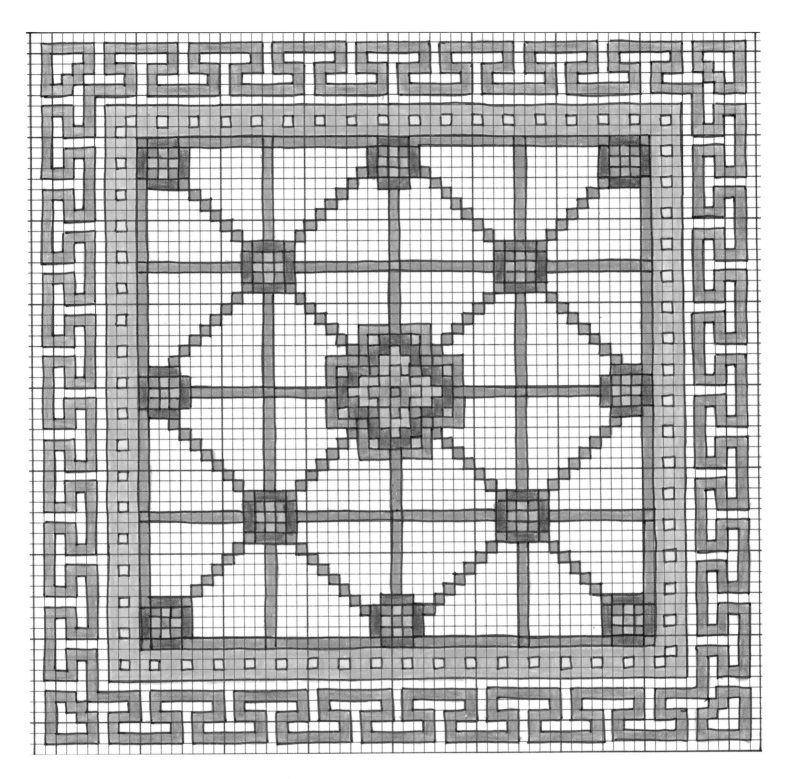

*One square on the chart represents one cross
stitch sewn over two horizontal and two vertical
canvas threads.*

◆

NONG KHAI BRAIDS

Thailand has many woven textile designs which are used for fabrics and wide braids. These textiles are also made into cushions of a style unique to the north-east of the country. ❦ As in other Asian countries, the Thai people sometimes tie-dye the threads *before* weaving to create a multicoloured effect. In this design I achieved a similar effect using one of the random-dyed knitting yarns which are now readily available. It gives a lively texture and introduces many colours into the design. The stripes of colour and texture add visual interest and the geometric design further reflects the traditional textiles of Thailand.

The geometric designs on the braids stacked up in displays form curious patterns, and the piles of triangular cushions create interesting designs.

Nong Khai Braids

FINISHED SIZE

$16\frac{1}{2} \times 16$in (42×41cm)

MATERIALS

$20\frac{1}{2} \times 20$in (51.5×50cm) of 10-mesh canvas
Size 18 needle
Persian 3-stranded yarn: six skeins of white; three each of green, pale pink, purple, blue and dark pink; two each of lemon and pale blue.
One ball of random-coloured knitting yarn.

STITCHING

Each square on the chart represents one horizontal canvas thread. Starting at one edge of the design, follow the embroidery row by row. Work the four colour bands of purple, pink, green and blue in straight stitch over two horizontal threads. Also work the geometric diamond design in straight stitch, following the chart. The wide, white bands are worked in web stitch which gives the impression of weaving. The central design is sewn in diamond eye stitch with random-dyed knitting yarn. (Instructions for all stitches are given in the stitch guide.)

This design could, of course, be increased to any size by adding extra rows of stripes.

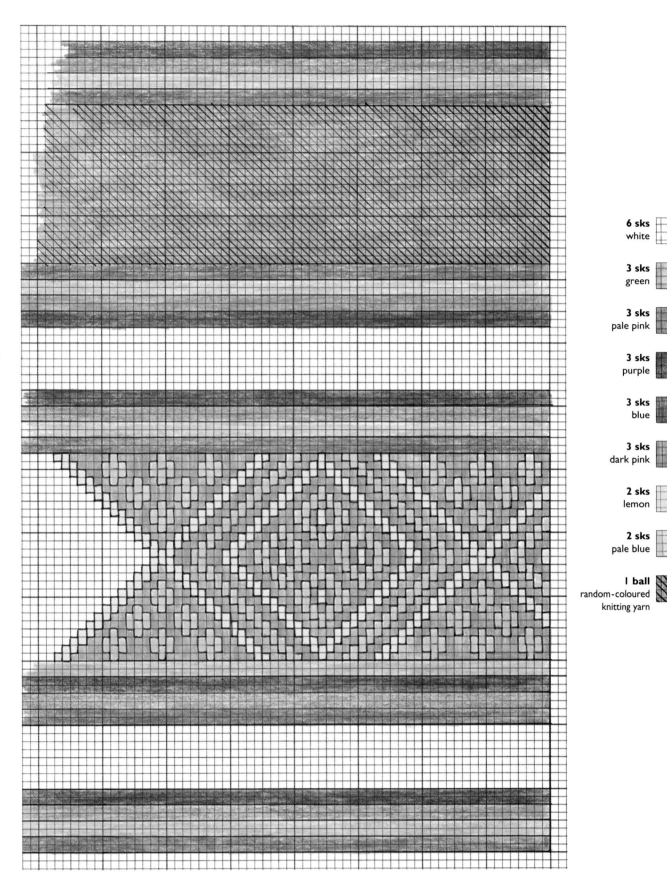

eye stitch

web stitch

web stitch

6 sks
white

3 sks
green

3 sks
pale pink

3 sks
purple

3 sks
blue

3 sks
dark pink

2 sks
lemon

2 sks
pale blue

1 ball
random-coloured
knitting yarn

One square in the chart represents a horizontal canvas thread covered by a vertical straight stitch.

FOURTEEN

SIGHTS AND SOUNDS OF INDIA

The main inspiration for this design came from the sounds of India, where an 'orchestra' of children, dogs, hens, cows, cars, bikes, rickshaws, street vendors and trains (to list but a few of the 'instruments') perpetually assaults one's ears. The design also evokes some of the antique embroidered hangings used for ceremonial purposes, which are made up of tiny, intricate patterns and mirror motifs. ❧ I tried to echo this random yet constant cacophony by repeating stars, circles and rectangles in striking, irregular patterns. A narrow brown stripe holds in this busy pattern, with just a few elements spilling onto the chequered border.

The infinite variety of colour, pattern and noise from all directions persists in heightening one's awareness of experiences in India.

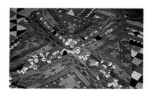

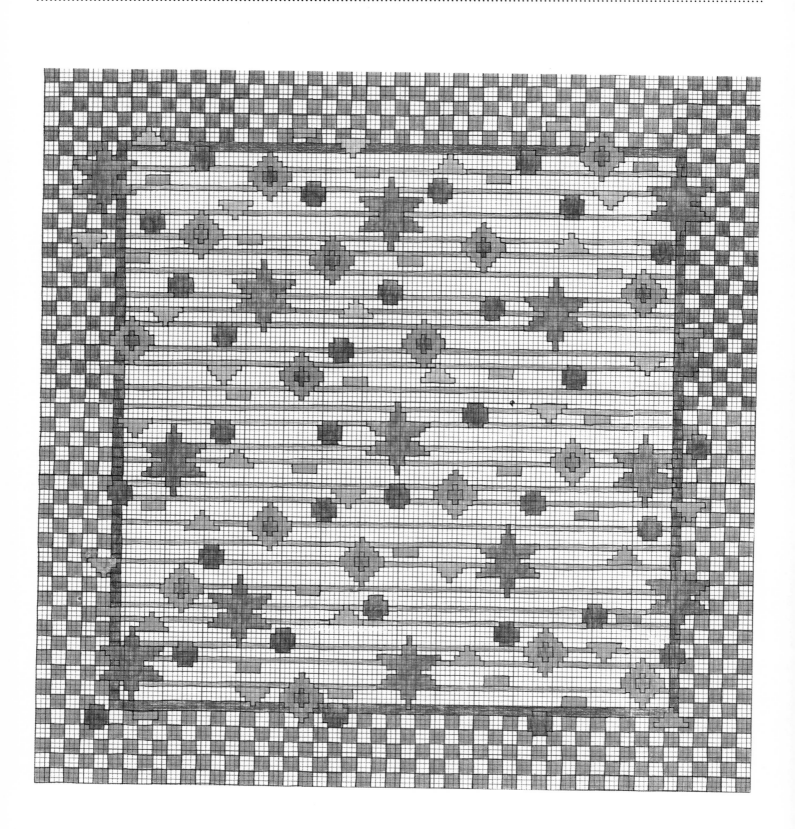

Each square in the chart represents one horizontal canvas thread covered by a vertical straight stitch.

SIGHTS AND SOUNDS OF INDIA

For red check border:

4 hks cream	
2 hks red	
3 sks brown	
3 sks bottle green	
2 sks purple	
2 sks pink	
2 sks pale blue	
2 sks putty	
I sk turquoise	
I sk violet	
I sk grass green	

For blue check border:

4 hks cream	
2 hks navy	
3 sks brown	
3 sks gold	
2 sks pink	
2 sks pale green	
2 sks lemon	
2 sks grass green	
I sk purple	
I sk turquoise	
I sk red	

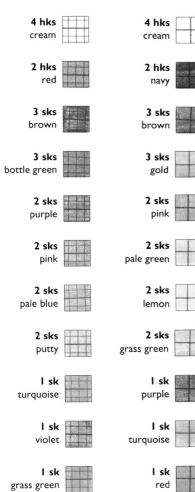

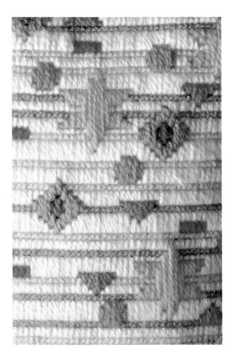

FINISHED SIZE

$14^{1}/_{2}$in (37cm) square

MATERIALS

$16^{1}/_{2}$in (42cm) square of 10-mesh canvas
Size 18 needle
Tapestry yarn (for red check border): four hanks of cream, two of red; the following skeins: three each of brown and bottle green; two each of purple, pink, pale blue and putty; one each of turquoise, violet and grass green.
Tapestry yarn (for blue check border): four hanks of cream, two of navy; the following skeins: three each of brown and gold; two each of pink, pale green, lemon and grass green; one each of purple, turquoise and red.

STITCHING

The design is worked throughout in vertical straight stitch. Following the chart, each square represents one horizontal canvas thread. The bottle green (or gold in the alternative colourway) star at the centre of the design provides a good starting point. When the star is complete, work outwards, stitching the horizontal lines of colour. Sew the other shapes when and where they interrupt the lines.

Build up the design in this way until the coloured lines and shapes in the centre panel are complete. Fill in the background with the cream wool. Sew the narrow brown stripe which encloses the design in straight stitch over two canvas threads. Complete the border by adding the chequered design of three straight stitches worked over three canvas threads.

FIFTEEN

ORISSA CROCODILES

My journey took me to Orissa to see the mystical Hindu temples on the sea-shores and the famous stone wall sculptures. From dawn to night, pupils at the schools of sculpture produce a constant tapping of picks on stone, creating the evocative sound of the region and resulting in fine, delicate carvings. ❧ I also went to see a crocodile farm, which provided a fascinating contrast to the intellectual and religious sights. The crocodiles were stacked one on top of the other, looking frozen in time and space, jaws menacingly open to regulate body temperature. You had to watch carefully to observe any signs of life, and this lack of motion was in sharp contrast to the hustle I'd got used to in India. ❧ I made a graphic drawing of a crocodile and interlocked four of them, like an Escher design, to recall the way they were piled up. You could therefore extend this design vertically to any depth, by adding more and more crocodiles.

*The crocodiles were almost as motionless as these
ancient stone wall carvings of Mahabalipuram, which have
given rise to many schools of sculpture in the area.*

ORISSA CROCODILES

FINISHED SIZE

14in (36cm) square

MATERIALS

16in (41cm) square of 12-mesh canvas
Size 20 needle

Tapestry yarn: Two hanks of black; three skeins each of pale yellow, emerald, pale emerald and pastel green; two skeins each of dark yellow and turquoise; one skein each of mid-yellow, pale blue, pale green, mid-green, dark green, pale pink, bright pink, magenta, pale purple, mid-purple and dark purple, and a few strands of white for the details (not shown on the colour key).

STITCHING

Transfer the line drawing onto the canvas using a soft pencil or pale felt-tip pen. The entire design is worked in tent stitch over one thread of canvas. Begin by sewing the black outlines to position the shapes. Once the black lines are complete, fill in the coloured areas, working one crocodile at a time. The different colour tones within each crocodile are indicated by the finer black lines on the chart.

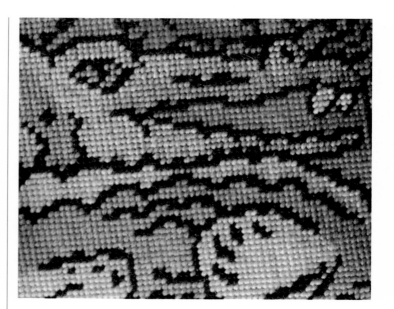

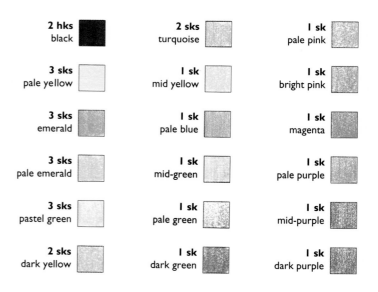

2 hks black	**2 sks** turquoise	**1 sk** pale pink
3 sks pale yellow	**1 sk** mid yellow	**1 sk** bright pink
3 sks emerald	**1 sk** pale blue	**1 sk** magenta
3 sks pale emerald	**1 sk** mid-green	**1 sk** pale purple
3 sks pastel green	**1 sk** pale green	**1 sk** mid-purple
2 sks dark yellow	**1 sk** dark green	**1 sk** dark purple

The design is worked in tent stitch throughout.
Only the thick black lines are to be stitched; the
narrow black lines are for guidance alone, to
mark the change of colours.

SIXTEEN

FIRE DRAGON

The dragon motif features significantly in Buddhist temples and Nepalese paintings, known as 'thangkas'. Their twisted bodies coil up and a blaze of fire pours from their nostrils and mouths. Block prints of dragons and other Nepalese, Tibetan and Chinese deities are made on locally produced rice paper. When the flimsy paper is held up to the light, the dragons become very real and threatening, as if floating in space. ❧ The dragons particularly attracted me for their simplicity of design. Using mainly black and white, I added some soft colours for subtlety. The gold adds sparkle and sets off the shape and movement of the body. I based the border on the 'everlasting line' motif, which also features in Nepalese religious symbolism. I liked the combination of the moving, twisting figure and the static border. It makes the dragon appear to be breaking out of its boundaries and emphasizes its power.

The powerful images of dragons fascinated me: the apparently simple geometric patterns proved to be sophisticated and complex designs that used continuous lines.

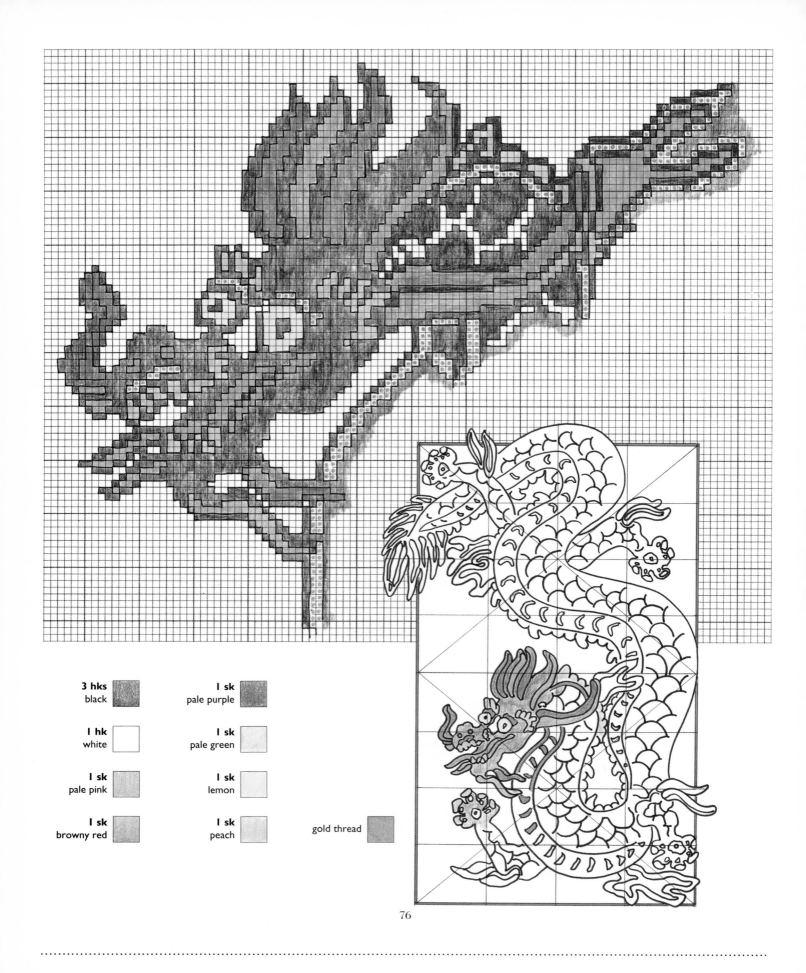

3 hks
black

I sk
pale purple

I hk
white

I sk
pale green

I sk
pale pink

I sk
lemon

I sk
browny red

I sk
peach

gold thread

FIRE DRAGON

FINISHED SIZE

15in × 22in (38cm × 56cm)

MATERIALS

20in × 25in (50cm × 64cm) of 12-mesh canvas
Size 20 needle
Tapestry yarn: three hanks of black; one hank each of white and red; one skein each of pale pink, browny red, pale purple, pale green, lemon, peach.
Gold thread; red metallic thread
Coton perlé 5 (pearl cotton): eight 27³/₈yd (25m) skeins of white.

STITCHING

The dragon is shown as a line drawing on a grid, with each square of the grid representing 2in (5cm). Draw an area 8 × 16in (20.5 × 41cm) in the centre of your canvas.

Scale up the picture of the dragon, square by square, onto the canvas.

Working the dragon in tent stitch, begin by sewing the black areas and then add the other colours and the gold. A chart of the dragon's head has been provided on which each square represents one tent stitch.

Once the dragon is complete you can begin the border. Follow the charts for the corner motifs (turning the charts upside down for the top two corners). Sew the solid centre of the border in red tapestry yarn using diagonal stitch for a lovely cushioned effect. On either side, work a single line of tent stitch in red metallic thread.

Next, fill in the background with cross stitch, over two horizontal and two vertical canvas threads, using white coton perlé 5 (pearl cotton). This gives a light and shiny effect to contrast with the dragon's body.

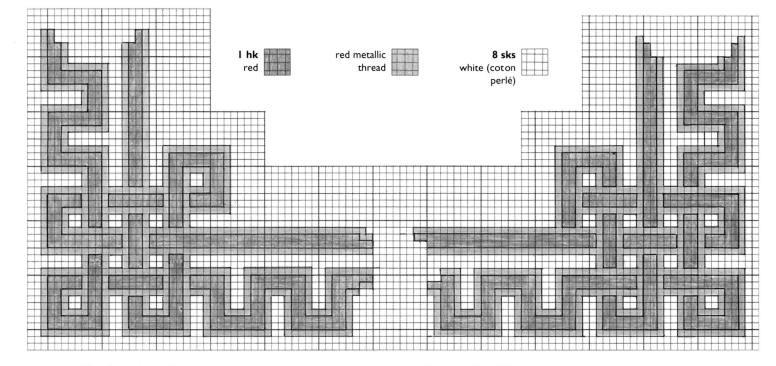

The chart shows the border design which uses tent stitch in the metallic thread and diagonal stitch for the red tapestry yarn.
Each square represents the intersecting canvas threads.

WOVEN DIAMONDS

This sophisticated and intricate design is a traditional Thai weaving pattern made up of diamonds repeated in regular formation. The design can therefore be extended to any size, and can be either rectangular or square. The patterns within the diamonds are symmetrical, and once you have grasped the workings of the pattern it becomes very easy to follow. ✤ I created this design by adapting elements from textile patterns which I saw being woven on ancient wooden looms.

*I broke down this complex woven design into a pattern
that can easily be sewn in straight stitch on canvas.*

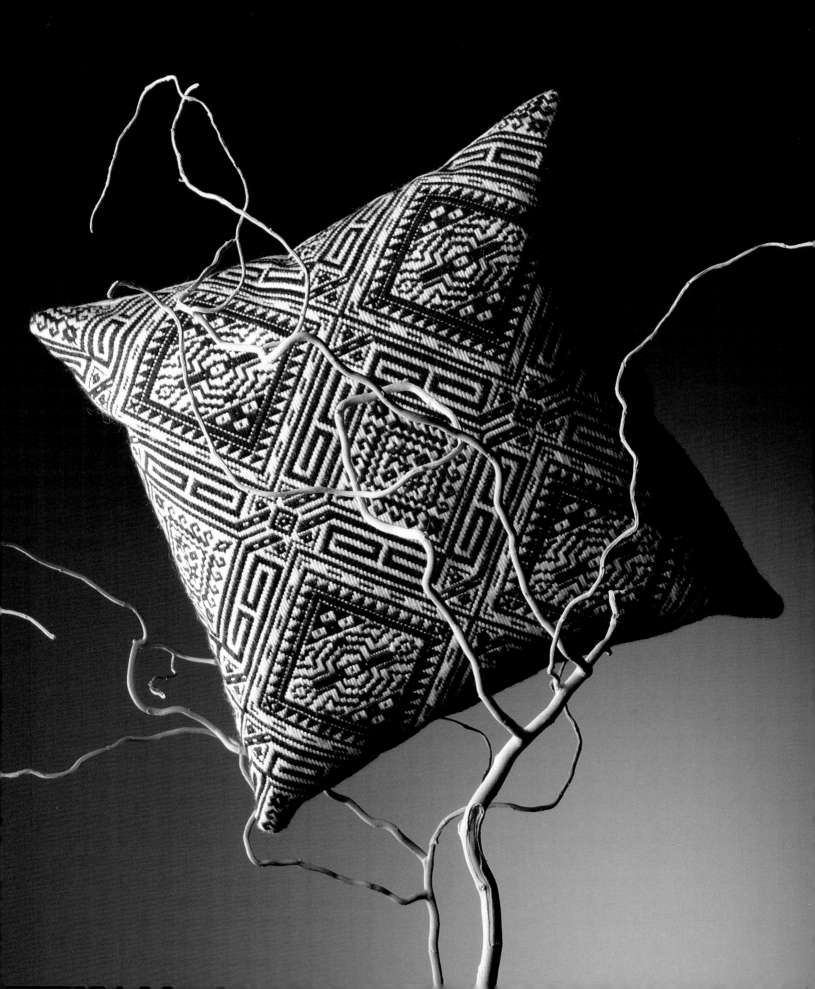

3 hks
navy blue

3 hks
cream

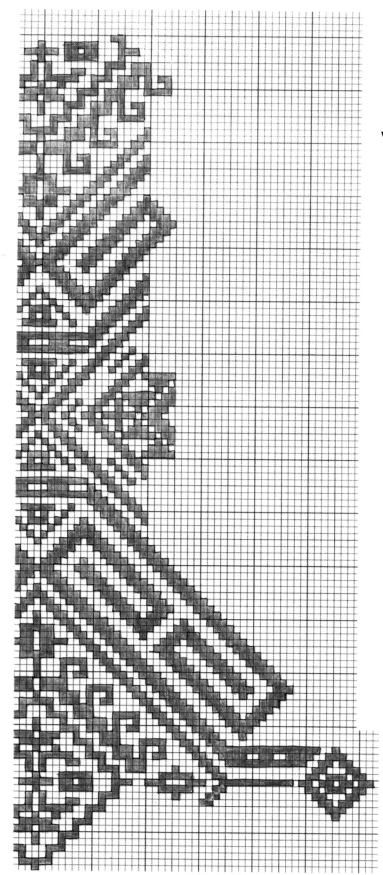

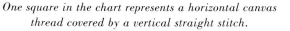

WOVEN DIAMONDS

FINISHED SIZE

17in (43cm) square

MATERIALS

19in (48cm) square of 12-mesh canvas
Size 20 needle
Tapestry yarn: three hanks each of navy blue
and cream.

STITCHING

The design is worked entirely in straight stitch
over varying numbers of threads. Each square
on the chart represents one horizontal canvas
thread. Starting at the centre and working in
navy blue only, sew the central diamond
design. Build up the design by stitching the
surrounding diamonds and pattern. Fill in the
remaining areas with cream wool.

*One square in the chart represents a horizontal canvas
thread covered by a vertical straight stitch.*

CHINESE CHEQUERS

Malaysia is a wonderful pot-pourri of different races, religions and cultures and this design is based on some of the Chinese influences visible in the country. ❦ Chinese chequers is a very popular game played by children and adults, and the simple star motif forms the central feature of this rug. To make the rug more decorative, I developed the Chinese theme by using the circular yin and yang symbol, which features in Buddhist temples. This symbol embodies the balance of all things – both positive and negative – and in itself is a very pleasing graphic image. A traditional Chinese border using the everlasting line forms the top and bottom edges. ❦ The design shown here is a rug, but the rectangular shape would lend itself to a set of table mats. For a mat, use a smaller mesh canvas and a finer yarn, such as silk or coton à broder (soft cotton). The rug and the mats can also be used to play Chinese chequers!

HOW TO PLAY CHINESE CHEQUERS

The game is for two to six players. Each player has ten counters placed on the ten dark brown dots in one of the large triangles. Use buttons in each of the six colours: green, pink, lemon, pale green, blue and mauve, or sew the centre of plain buttons with each of the different yarns.

The object of the game is to move your counters, one dot at a time, across the star to the opposite triangle. The players take it in turn to move their counters from one tan dot to the next. Quicker moves can be made by jumping over another player's counter to the next available dot. You can make several jumps at a time, but only over one counter at a time. The moves can be made in any direction. The first player to transfer all his counters to the opposite triangle is the winner.